## Get updated: The must-know events, trends, and technology

The eighth edition update includes the latest media developments and coverage of the political, economic, and cultural issues affecting our mass media and culture today.

▶ A new Extended Case Study, "How the News Media Covered the News Corp. Scandal," takes a critical look at how the news media investigated the stories that emerged from the salacious News Corp. phone hacking scandal — like just how much Rupert Murdoch *actually* knew (pp. 509–516).

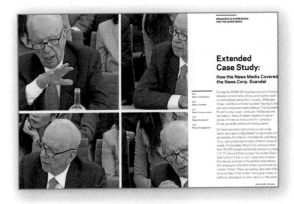

▶ A new discussion of the Occupy Wall Street movement and what the media — new and old — are saying about it in Chapter 1 (pp. 3–4).

▶ A look at the Arab Spring revolutions and the role Twitter and Facebook played in galvanizing protestors and communicating what was happening on a local and global level (p. 51).

▶ A new Chapter 7 opener discusses whether tablet-only papers, like the *Daily*, can help save the lagging newspaper industry (pp. 219–220).

▶ Updated discussions on the battle for viewers' loyalty (and dollars) between cable companies and streaming television services in Chapter 5 (pp. 171–172).

▶ A look at Al Jazeera English and why we can't watch it on more cable systems in Chapter 13 (p. 441).

▶ A new Chapter 10 opener explores iAd and the rapidly growing potential of mobile advertising (pp. 319–320).

# Praise for Media & Culture

*Media & Culture* is a solid, thorough, and interesting text. I will be a stronger mass communication instructor for having read this text.

MYLEEA D. HILL,
*ARKANSAS STATE UNIVERSITY*

*Media & Culture* is the best survey text of the current crop. The writing is well constructed and does not talk down to the students.

STEVE MILLER,
*RUTGERS UNIVERSITY*

*Media & Culture*'s critical approach to the history, theory, economy, technology, and regulation of the various mass media helps students become critical users of the media.

SHIO NAM,
*UNIVERSITY OF NORTH FLORIDA*

*Media & Culture* is media literacy meets mass communication— it really connects the two, something we should all be focusing on.

WENDY NELSON,
*PALOMAR COLLEGE*

I think the Campbell text is out-standing. It is a long-overdue media text that is grounded in pressing questions about American culture and its connection to the techniques and institutions of commercial communication. It is, indeed, an important book. At the undergraduate level, that's saying something.

STEVE M. BARKIN,
*UNIVERSITY OF MARYLAND*

*Media & Culture* respects students' opinions, while challenging them to take more responsibility and to be accountable for their media choices. This text is essential for professors who are truly committed to teaching students how to understand the media.

DREW JACOBS,
*CAMDEN COUNTY COLLEGE*

The critical perspective has enlightened the perspective of all of us who study media, and Campbell has the power to infect students with his love of the subject.

ROGER DESMOND,
*UNIVERSITY OF HARTFORD*

I will switch to Campbell because it is a tour de force of coverage and interpretation, it is the best survey text in the field hands down, and it challenges students. Campbell's text is the most thorough and complete in the field. . . . No other text is even close.

RUSSELL BARCLAY,
*QUINNIPIAC UNIVERSITY*

The feature boxes are excellent and are indispensable to any classroom.

MARVIN WILLIAMS,
*KINGSBOROUGH
COMMUNITY COLLEGE*

I love *Media & Culture*! I have used it since the first edition. *Media & Culture* integrates the history of a particular medium or media concept with the culture, economics, and the technological advances of the time. But more than that, the authors are explicit in their philosophy that media and culture cannot be separated.

DEBORAH LARSON,
*MISSOURI STATE UNIVERSITY*

# Media & Culture

## An Introduction to Mass Communication

Eighth Edition

2013 Update

**Richard Campbell**
Miami University

**Christopher R. Martin**
University of Northern Iowa

**Bettina Fabos**
University of Northern Iowa

**BEDFORD/ST. MARTIN'S**
Boston • New York

**For Bedford/St. Martin's**

*Publisher for Communication:* Erika Gutierrez
*Developmental Editor:* Ada Fung Platt
*Production Editor:* Peter Jacoby
*Production Supervisor:* Andrew Ensor
*Marketing Manager:* Stacey Propps
*Copy Editor:* Denise Quirk
*Indexer:* Sandi Schroeder
*Photo Researcher:* Sue McDermott
*Permissions Manager:* Kalina K. Ingham
*Art Director:* Lucy Krikorian
*Text and Cover Design:* TODA (The Office of Design and Architecture)
*Cover Art:* Digitized art by TODA based on an original photograph by datarec
*Composition:* Cenveo Publisher Services
*Printing and Binding:* RR Donnelley and Sons

*President:* Joan E. Feinberg
*Editorial Director:* Denise B. Wydra
*Director of Development:* Erica T. Appel
*Director of Marketing:* Karen R. Soeltz
*Director of Production:* Susan W. Brown
*Associate Director, Editorial Production:* Elise S. Kaiser
*Managing Editor:* Shuli Traub

Library of Congress Control Number: 2011940050

Manufactured in the United States of America.

7 6 5 4 3 2
f e d c b a

*For information,* write: Bedford/St. Martin's, 75 Arlington Street,
Boston, MA 02116    (617-399-4000)

ISBN: 978-1-4576-0491-1

**"WE ARE NOT ALONE."**
*For my family — Chris, Caitlin, and Dianna*


**"YOU MAY SAY I'M A DREAMER,
BUT I'M NOT THE ONLY ONE."**
*For our daughters — Olivia and Sabine*

# About the Authors

**Richard Campbell**, director of the journalism program at Miami University, is the author of *"60 Minutes" and the News: A Mythology for Middle America* (1991) and coauthor of *Cracked Coverage: Television News, the Anti-Cocaine Crusade, and the Reagan Legacy* (1994). Campbell has written for numerous publications, including *Columbia Journalism Review, Journal of Communication*, and *Media Studies Journal*, and he is on the editorial boards of *Critical Studies in Mass Communication* and *Television Quarterly*. He holds a Ph.D. from Northwestern University and has also taught at the University of Wisconsin-Milwaukee, Mount Mary College, the University of Michigan, and Middle Tennessee State University.

**Christopher R. Martin** is a professor of journalism at the University of Northern Iowa and author of *Framed! Labor and the Corporate Media* (2003). He has written articles and reviews on journalism, televised sports, the Internet, and labor for several publications, including *Communication Research, Journal of Communication, Journal of Communication Inquiry, Labor Studies Journal*, and *Culture, Sport, and Society*. He is also on the editorial board of the *Journal of Communication Inquiry*. Martin holds a Ph.D. from the University of Michigan and has also taught at Miami University.

**Bettina Fabos**, an award-winning video maker and former print reporter, is an associate professor of visual communication and interactive media studies at the University of Northern Iowa. She is the author of *Wrong Turn on the Information Superhighway: Education and the Commercialized Internet* (2004). Her areas of expertise include critical media literacy, Internet commercialization, the role of the Internet in education, and media representations of popular culture. Her work has been published in *Library Trends, Review of Educational Research*, and *Harvard Educational Review*. Fabos has also taught at Miami University and has a Ph.D. from the University of Iowa.

# Brief Contents

# Preface

It's no secret that the media are in a constant state of flux and changing faster than ever. In 2011, Amazon.com reported that e-books were outselling print books, iTunes App Store downloads hit the 18 billion mark–surpassing music downloads–and Twitter reached 100 million active users worldwide. And with every new device expected to multitask as an e-reader, a music player, a TV and movie screen, a gaming system, and a phone, convergence is the hottest topic in the media industries and in mass communication classrooms across the country.

Today's students are experiencing these fast and furious developments firsthand. Many now watch television shows on their own schedule rather than when they are broadcast on TV, stream hit singles rather than purchase full albums, and use their videogame consoles to watch movies and socialize with friends. But while students are familiar with the newest products and latest formats, they may not understand how the media evolved to this point, or what all these developments mean. This is why we believe the critical and cultural perspectives at the core of *Media and Culture's* approach are more important than ever. *Media and Culture* pulls back the curtain to show students how the media really work–from the historical roots and economics of each media industry to the implications of today's consolidated media ownership. And by learning to look at the media–whether "old" or "new"–through a critical lens, students will better understand the complex relationship between the mass media and our shared culture and become informed critics.

The eighth edition of *Media and Culture* confronts head-on the realities of how we consume media *now*. First, with cable networks encroaching on broadcast networks' turf by producing quality original programming, and with the growing number of both broadcast and cable shows available on the Internet, the line between cable and broadcast television is increasingly blurred. To better reflect this change, *Media and Culture* weaves together the histories and trends of traditional broadcast and cable along with a discussion of third-screen technologies in the new Chapter 5, "Television and Cable: The Power of Visual Culture." Second, as the popularity of online gaming continues to grow, and as videogame consoles morph into all-in-one media centers with social networking and video streaming capabilities, video games are now an active part of mass media. New coverage of the economics, impact, and future of video games in Chapter 2, "The Internet, Digital Media, and Media Convergence," addresses the increasingly larger role that gaming plays in the media.

In addition to reflecting such larger shifts in the media landscape, we have added new dedicated sections on media convergence in each industry chapter (Chapters 2-9) that go beyond telling students what they already know about the latest media devices. Discussions of such topics as the impact of music streaming on the recording industry's profits (Chapter 3) and how magazine content has evolved for tablets like the iPad (Chapter 8) help students understand how convergence has changed the ways media are created, distributed, financed, and consumed. And now, with the eighth edition update, *Media and Culture* continues to make the complex nature of media accessible to students through the use of the most current examples and stories.

Of course, *Media and Culture* retains its well-loved and teachable organization that gives students a clear understanding of the historical and cultural contexts for each media industry. And to help engage students immediately, each chapter now begins with a bulleted list that previews upcoming key points and critical-thinking questions that encourage students to consider their own media experiences before delving into the chapter content.

Our signature approach to studying the media has struck a chord with hundreds of instructors and thousands of students across the United States and North America. Not only has *Media and Culture* become a widely admired learning tool, but it also remains the best-selling introductory text for this course. We would like to take a moment and express our gratitude to all the teachers and students who have supported *Media and Culture* over the years. We continue to be enthusiastic about–and humbled by–the chance to work with the amazing community of teachers that has developed around *Media and Culture*. We hope the text enables students to become more knowledgeable media consumers and engaged, media-literate citizens with a critical stake in shaping our dynamic world.

## The Eighth Edition Update: The Most Current—and Media-Savvy—Text Available

What a difference a year makes. Since the eighth edition was published, we watched the Arab Spring uprisings unfold in squares and streets–and over YouTube, Twitter, and Facebook. We breathlessly followed coverage of the News Corp. phone hacking scandal. And we witnessed Americans express their frustrations with the weak economy in the Occupy Wall Street protests in cities and towns all across the United States. And with convergence changing the ways we create, finance, distribute, and consume *all* media, understanding the complex interplay between the media and our culture is more important than ever. And so, with the eighth edition update, we do more than name-check current events and trends. We demonstrate to students the centrality of media in our lives, and help them become informed media consumers, by showing them how to critically analyze the media events they are living through right now.

- **An in-depth analysis of the fallout from the News Corp. phone hacking scandal,** covered in the new Extended Case Study, "How the News Media Covered the News. Corp Scandal," shows students how to use the critical process to investigate the stories that emerged in the news media from the scandal–from the degree of Rupert Murdoch's involvement to the cozy relationship between government and Big Media. By examining how the news media covered this media scandal, students will gain a greater understanding of the news media's role as watchdog.
- **New chapter openers examine the latest trends and developments,** including the growing Occupy Wall Street movement and how the media–old and new–are covering it, the potential of tablet-only newspapers like the *Daily* to revive the declining newspaper industry, the exponential growth of mobile advertising, and the *Huffington Post*-AOL merger as part of the ongoing trend of technology companies investing in content development.
- **New feature boxes analyze current media issues** such as the role that social media played in galvanizing Arab Spring protestors and communicating their stories around the world, the perception of Al Jazeera English in the United States, and the effects of violence and misogyny in hyperrealistic video games like *Red Dead Redemption*.
- **Updated and expanded coverage throughout** ensures that *Media and Culture* has the most relevant content available. In addition to up-to-date statistics and economic information, the eighth edition update includes insightful analysis of such topics as cloud-basic music services and their impact on the recording industry, the continuing growth of third- and fourth-screen technologies, the explosion of gaming on mobile devices, the *New York Times*' paywall, and the FCC's separate net neutrality rules for fixed broadband and wireless networks.

## The Eighth Edition

The eighth edition keeps pace with today's rapidly changing media landscape with new coverage of the technological, economic, and social effects of media convergence across all the media industries, truly reflecting how we consume media in a converged world.

- **Combined coverage of television, cable and third-screen technologies in Chapter 5 fully reflects how we watch television today.** In addition to merging the histories and trends of broadcast and cable, the eighth edition includes new coverage of such third-screen technology as Internet video streaming and TV programming on smartphones and touchscreen devices.
- **New discussion of video games in Chapter 2 recognizes their larger role in the mass media.** The eighth edition explores how the Internet helped make that transition possible, and examines how gaming consoles now function as convergence centers, allowing players to browse the Web, watch videos, and interact with friends.
- **Dedicated sections in every industry chapter explore the larger implications of media convergence.** *Media and Culture* goes beyond simply telling students about the latest media technologies. The eighth edition analyzes the social and economic impact of these developments—from how the publishing industry is adapting to e-books and digital readers to how filmmakers are harnessing the power of social media to promote their movies.
- **Engaging students from the start, new chapter-opening bulleted lists introduce upcoming key concepts and help students focus their reading.** In addition, new critical-thinking questions encourage students to consider their own media experiences.

## The Best and Broadest Introduction to the Mass Media

- **A critical approach to media literacy.** *Media and Culture* introduces students to five stages of the critical thinking and writing process—description, analysis, interpretation, evaluation, and engagement. The text uses these stages as a lens for examining the historical context and current processes that shape mass media as part of our culture. This framework informs the writing throughout, including the Media Literacy and the Critical Process boxes in each chapter.
- **A cultural perspective.** The text consistently focuses on the vital relationship between mass media and our shared culture—how cultural trends influence the mass media and how specific historical developments, technical innovations, and key decision makers in the history of the media have affected the ways our democracy and society have evolved.
- **Comprehensive coverage.** The text gives students the nuts-and-bolts content they need to understand each media industry's history, organizational structure, economic models, and market statistics.
- **An exploration of media economics and democracy.** To become more engaged in our society and more discerning as consumers, students must pay attention to the complex relationship between democracy and capitalism. To that end, *Media and Culture* spotlights the significance and impact of multinational media systems throughout the text, including the media ownership snapshots in each of the industry chapters. It also invites students to explore the implications of the Telecommunications Act of 1996 and other deregulation resolutions. Additionally, each chapter ends with a discussion of the effects of various mass media on the nature of democratic life.
- **Compelling storytelling.** Most mass media make use of storytelling to tap into our shared beliefs and values, and so does *Media and Culture*. Each chapter presents the events and issues surrounding media culture as intriguing and informative narratives, rather than as a series of unconnected facts and feats, and maps the uneasy and parallel changes in consumer culture and democratic society.
- **The most accessible book available.** Learning tools in every chapter help students find and remember the information they need to know. New bulleted lists at the

beginning of every chapter give students a road map to key concepts; annotated time-lines offer powerful visual guides that highlight key events and refer to more coverage in the chapter; Media Literacy and the Critical Process boxes model the five-step process; and the Chapter Reviews help students study and review.

## Student Resources

For more information on the student resources or to learn about package options, please visit the online catalog at **bedfordstmartins.com/mediaculture/catalog.**

### Expanded! *MassCommClass for Media and Culture* at yourmasscommclass.com

*MassCommClass* is designed to support students in all aspects of the introduction to mass communication course. It's fully loaded with the *Media and Culture e-Book,* videos from *VideoCentral: Mass Communication,* the Online Image Library, the *Media Career Guide,* and multiple study aids. Even better, new functionality makes it easy to upload and annotate video, embed YouTube clips, and create video assignments for individual students, groups, or the whole class. Adopt *MassCommClass* and get all the premium content and tools in one fully customizable course space; then assign, rearrange, and mix our resources with yours. *Mass-CommClass* requires an activation code.

### Book Companion Site at bedfordstmartins.com/mediaculture

Free study aids on the book's Web site help students gauge their understanding of the text material through concise chapter summaries with study questions, visual activities that combine images and critical-thinking analysis, and pre- and post-chapter quizzes to help students assess their strengths and weaknesses and focus their studying. Students can also keep current on media news with streaming headlines from a variety of news sources and can use the Media Portal to find the best media-related Web sites. In addition, students can access other online resources such as *VideoCentral: Mass Communication* and the *Media and Culture e-Book.*

### *VideoCentral: Mass Communication* at bedfordstmartins.com/mediaculture

With over forty clips, this growing collection of short videos gives students an inside look at the media industries through the eyes of leading professionals. Each three- to five-minute clip discusses issues such as the future of print media, net neutrality, media convergence, and media ownership. The videos contain unique commentary from *Media and Culture* author Richard Campbell, as well as some of the biggest names in media–including Amy Goodman, Clarence Page, Junot Díaz, and Anne Rice. *VideoCentral: Mass Communication* can be packaged for free with the print book.

### *Media and Culture e-Book* and digital options

The Bedford e-Book for *Media and Culture* includes the same content as the print book and allows students to add their own notes and highlight important information. Instructors can customize the e-book by adding their own content and deleting or rearranging chapters. A variety of other digital versions of *Media and Culture* are available that can be used on comput-ers, tablets, or e-readers. For more information, see **bedfordstmartins.com/ebooks.**

### *Media Career Guide: Preparing for Jobs in the 21st Century,* Eighth Edition

Sherri Hope Culver, *Temple University;* James Seguin, *Robert Morris College;*
ISBN: 978-0-312-54260-3

Practical, student-friendly, and revised with recent trends in the job market (like the role of social media in a job search), this guide includes a comprehensive directory of media jobs, practical tips, and career guidance for students who are considering a major in the media industries. The *Media Career Guide* can also be packaged for free with the print book.

# Instructor Resources

For more information or to order or download the instructor resources, please visit the online catalog at **bedfordstmartins.com/mediaculture/catalog.**

## Instructor's Resource Manual

Bettina Fabos, *University of Northern Iowa;* Christopher R. Martin, *University of Northern Iowa;* and Shawn Harmsen, *University of Iowa*

This downloadable manual improves on what has always been the best and most comprehensive instructor teaching tool available for the introduction to mass communication courses. This extensive resource provides a range of teaching approaches, tips for facilitating in-class discussions, writing assignments, outlines, lecture topics, lecture spin-offs, critical-process exercises, classroom media resources, and an annotated list of more than two hundred video resources.

## Test Bank

Christopher R. Martin, *University of Northern Iowa;* Bettina Fabos, *University of Northern Iowa;* and Shawn Harmsen, *University of Iowa*

Available both in print and as software formatted for Windows and Macintosh, the Test Bank includes multiple choice, true/false, matching, fill-in-the-blank, and short and long essay questions for every chapter in *Media and Culture.*

## PowerPoint Slides

PowerPoint presentations to help guide your lecture are available for downloading for each chapter in *Media and Culture.*

## The Online Image Library for *Media and Culture*

This free instructor resource provides access to hundreds of dynamic images from the pages of *Media and Culture.* These images can be easily incorporated into lectures or used to spark in-class discussion.

## *VideoCentral: Mass Communication* DVD

The instructor DVD for *VideoCentral: Mass Communication* gives you another convenient way to access the collection of over forty short video clips from leading media professionals. The DVD is available upon adoption of *VideoCentral: Mass Communication;* please contact your local sales representative.

## *About the Media: Video Clips DVD to Accompany Media and Culture*

This free instructor resource includes over fifty media-related clips, keyed to every chapter in *Media and Culture.* Designed to be used as a discussion starter in the classroom or to illustrate examples from the textbook, this DVD provides the widest array of clips available for introduction to mass communication courses in a single resource. Selections include historical footage of the radio, television, and advertising industries; film from the Media Education Foundation; and other private and public domain materials. The DVD is available upon adoption of *Media and Culture;* please contact your local sales representative.

## Questions for Classroom Response Systems

Questions for every chapter in *Media and Culture* help integrate the latest classroom response systems (such as i>clicker) into your lecture to get instant feedback on students' understanding of course concepts as well as their opinions and perspectives.

## Content for Course Management Systems

Instructors can access content specifically designed for *Media and Culture* like quizzing and activities for course management systems such as WebCT and Blackboard. Visit **bedfordstmartins.com/coursepacks** for more information.

### The Bedford/St. Martin's Video Resource Library

Qualified instructors are eligible to receive videos from the resource library upon adoption of the text. The resource library includes full-length films; documentaries from Michael Moore, Bill Moyers, and Ken Burns; and news-show episodes from *Frontline* and *Now*. Please contact your local publisher's representative for more information.

## Acknowledgments

We are very grateful to everyone at Bedford/St. Martin's who supported this project through its many stages. We wish that every textbook author could have the kind of experience we had with these people: Chuck Christensen, Joan Feinberg, Denise Wydra, Erika Gutierrez, Erica Appel, Adrienne Petsick, Stacey Propps, Simon Glick, and Noel Hohnstine. Over the years, we have also collaborated with superb and supportive developmental editors: on the eighth edition update, Ada Fung Platt. We particularly appreciate the tireless work of Shuli Traub, managing editor, who oversaw the book's extremely tight schedule; Peter Jacoby, project editor, who kept the book on schedule while making sure we got the details right; Andy Ensor, production supervisor; and Dennis J. Conroy, senior production supervisor. Thanks also to TODA and Donna Dennison for a fantastic cover and interior design, and to Pelle Cass for a striking brochure. We are especially grateful to our research assistant, Susan Coffin, who functioned as a one-person clipping service throughout the process. We would also like to thank Shawn Harmsen, for his great work on updating the Instructor's Resource Manual and Test Bank.

We also want to thank the many fine and thoughtful reviewers who contributed ideas to the eighth edition of *Media and Culture*: Frank A. Aycock, *Appalachian State University*; Carrie Buchanan, *John Carroll University*; Lisa M. Burns, *Quinnipiac University*; Rich Cameron, *Cerritos College*; Katherine Foss, *Middle Tennessee State University*; Myleea D. Hill, *Arkansas State University*; Sarah Alford Hock, *Santa Barbara City College*; Sharon R. Hollenback, *Syracuse University*; Drew Jacobs, *Camden County College*; Susan Katz, *University of Bridgeport*; John Kerezy, *Cuyahoga Community College*; Les Kozaczek, *Franklin Pierce University*; Deborah L. Larson, *Missouri State University*; Susan Charles Lewis, *Minnesota State University-Mankato*; Rick B. Marks, *College of Southern Nevada*; Donna R. Munde, *Mercer County Community College*; Wendy Nelson, *Palomar College*; Charles B. Scholz, *New Mexico State University*; Don W. Stacks, *University of Miami*; Carl Sessions Stepp, *University of Maryland*; David Strukel, *University of Toledo*; Lisa Turowski, *Towson University*; Lisa M. Weidman, *Linfield College*.

For the seventh edition: Robert Blade, *Florida Community College*; Lisa Boragine, *Cape Cod Community College*; Joseph Clark, *University of Toledo*; Richard Craig, *San Jose State University*; Samuel Ebersole, *Colorado State University-Pueblo*; Brenda Edgerton-Webster, *Mississippi State University*; Tim Edwards, *University of Arkansas at Little Rock*; Mara Einstein, *Queens College*; Lillie M. Fears, *Arkansas State University*; Connie Fletcher, *Loyola University*; Monica Flippin-Wynn, *University of Oklahoma*; Gil Fowler, *Arkansas State University*; Donald G. Godfrey, *Arizona State University*; Patricia Homes, *University of Southwestern Louisiana*; Daniel McDonald, *Ohio State University*; Connie McMahon, *Barry University*; Steve Miller, *Rutgers University*; Siho Nam, *University of North Florida*; David Nelson, *University of Colorado-Colorado Springs*; Zengjun Peng, *St. Cloud State University*; Deidre Pike, *University of Nevada-Reno*; Neil Ralston, *Western Kentucky University*; Mike Reed, *Saddleback College*; David Roberts, *Missouri Valley College*; Donna Simmons, *California State University-Bakersfield*; Marc Skinner, *University of Idaho*; Michael Stamm, *University of Minnesota*; Bob Trumpbour, *Penn State University*; Kristin Watson, *Metro State University*; Jim Weaver, *Virginia Polytechnic and State University*; David Whitt, *Nebraska Wesleyan University*.

For the sixth edition: Boyd Dallos, *Lake Superior College*; Roger George, *Bellevue Community College*; Osvaldo Hirschmann, *Houston Community College*; Ed Kanis, *Butler University*; Dean A Kruckeberg, *University of Northern Iowa*; Larry Leslie, *University of South Florida*; Lori Liggett, *Bowling Green State University*; Steve Miller, *Rutgers University*; Robert Pondillo, *Middle Tennessee State University*; David Silver, *University of San Francisco*; Chris White, *Sam Houston State University*; Marvin Williams, *Kingsborough Community College*.

For the fifth edition: Russell Barclay, *Quinnipiac University*; Kathy Battles, *University of Michigan*; Kenton Bird, *University of Idaho*; Ed Bonza, *Kennesaw State University*; Larry L. Burris, *Middle Tennessee State University*; Ceilidh Charleson-Jennings, *Collin County Community College*; Raymond Eugene Costain, *University of Central Florida*; Richard Craig, *San Jose State University*; Dave Deeley, *Truman State University*; Janine Gerzanics, *West Valley College*; Beth Haller, *Towson University*; Donna Hemmila, *Diablo Valley College*; Sharon Hollenback, *Syracuse University*; Marshall D. Katzman, *Bergen Community College*; Kimberly Lauffer, *Towson University*; Steve Miller, *Rutgers University*; Stu Minnis, *Virginia Wesleyan College*; Frank G. Perez, *University of Texas at El Paso*; Dave Perlmutter, *Louisiana State University-Baton Rouge*; Karen Pitcher, *University of Iowa*; Ronald C. Roat, *University of Southern Indiana*; Marshel Rossow, *Minnesota State University*; Roger Saathoff, *Texas Tech University*; Matthew Smith, *Wittenberg University*; Marlane C. Steinwart, *Valparaiso University*.

For the fourth edition: Fay Y. Akindes, *University of Wisconsin-Parkside*; Robert Arnett, *Mississippi State University*; Charles Aust, *Kennesaw State University*; Russell Barclay, *Quinnipiac University*; Bryan Brown, *Southwest Missouri State University*; Peter W. Croisant, *Geneva College*; Mark Goodman, *Mississippi State University*; Donna Halper, *Emerson College*; Rebecca Self Hill, *University of Colorado*; John G. Hodgson, *Oklahoma State University*; Cynthia P. King, *American University*; Deborah L. Larson, *Southwest Missouri State University*; Charles Lewis, *Minnesota State University-Mankato*; Lila Lieberman, *Rutgers University*; Abbus Malek, *Howard University*; Anthony A. Olorunnisola, *Pennsylvania State University*; Norma Pecora, *Ohio University-Athens*; Elizabeth M. Perse, *University of Delaware*; Hoyt Purvis, *University of Arkansas*; Alison Rostankowski, *University of Wisconsin-Milwaukee*; Roger A. Soenksen, *James Madison University*; Hazel Warlaumont, *California State University-Fullerton*.

For the third edition: Gerald J. Baldasty, *University of Washington*; Steve M. Barkin, *University of Maryland*; Ernest L. Bereman, *Truman State University*; Daniel Bernadi, *University of Arizona*; Kimberly L. Bissell, *Southern Illinois University*; Audrey Boxmann, *Merrimack College*; Todd Chatman, *University of Illinois*; Ray Chavez, *University of Colorado*; Vic Costello, *Gardner-Webb University*; Paul D'Angelo, *Villanova University*; James Shanahan, *Cornell University*; Scott A. Webber, *University of Colorado*.

For the second edition: Susan B. Barnes, *Fordham University*; Margaret Bates, *City College of New York*; Steven Alan Carr, *Indiana University/Purdue University-Fort Wayne*; William G. Covington Jr., *Bridgewater State College*; Roger Desmond, *University of Hartford*; Jules d'Hemecourt, *Louisiana State University*; Cheryl Evans, *Northwestern Oklahoma State University*; Douglas Gomery, *University of Maryland*; Colin Gromatzky, *New Mexico State University*; John L. Hochheimer, *Ithaca College*; Sheena Malhotra, *University of New Mexico*; Sharon R. Mazzarella, *Ithaca College*; David Marc McCoy, *Kent State University*; Beverly Merrick, *New Mexico State University*; John Pantalone, *University of Rhode Island*; John Durham Peters, *University of Iowa*; Lisa Pieraccini, *Oswego State College*; Susana Powell, *Borough of Manhattan Community College*; Felicia Jones Ross, *Ohio State University*; Enid Sefcovic, *Florida Atlantic University*; Keith Semmel, *Cumberland College*; Augusta Simon, *Embry-Riddle Aeronautical University*; Clifford E. Wexler, *Columbia-Greene Community College*.

For the first edition: Paul Ashdown, *University of Tennessee*; Terry Bales, *Rancho Santiago College*; Russell Barclay, *Quinnipiac University*; Thomas Beell, *Iowa State University*; Fred

Blevens, *Southwest Texas State University*; Stuart Bullion, *University of Maine*; William G. Covington Jr., *Bridgewater State College*; Robert Daves, *Minneapolis Star Tribune*; Charles Davis, *Georgia Southern University*; Thomas Donahue, *Virginia Commonwealth University*; Ralph R. Donald, *University of Tennessee-Martin*; John P. Ferre, *University of Louisville*; Donald Fishman, *Boston College*; Elizabeth Atwood Gailey, *University of Tennessee*; Bob Gassaway, *University of New Mexico*; Anthony Giffard, *University of Washington*; Zhou He, *San Jose State University*; Barry Hollander, *University of Georgia*; Sharon Hollenbeck, *Syracuse University*; Anita Howard, *Austin Community College*; James Hoyt, *University of Wisconsin-Madison*; Joli Jensen, *University of Tulsa*; Frank Kaplan, *University of Colorado*; William Knowles, *University of Montana*; Michael Leslie, *University of Florida*; Janice Long, *University of Cincinnati*; Kathleen Maticheck, *Normandale Community College*; Maclyn McClary, *Humboldt State University*; Robert McGaughey, *Murray State University*; Joseph McKerns, *Ohio State University*; Debra Merskin, *University of Oregon*; David Morrissey, *Colorado State University*; Michael Murray, *University of Missouri at St. Louis*; Susan Dawson O'Brien, *Rose State College*; Patricia Bowie Orman, *University of Southern Colorado*; Jim Patton, *University of Arizona*; John Pauly, *St. Louis University*; Ted Pease, *Utah State University*; Janice Peck, *University of Colorado*; Tina Pieraccini, *University of New Mexico*; Peter Pringle, *University of Tennessee*; Sondra Rubenstein, *Hofstra University*; Jim St. Clair, *Indiana University Southeast*; Jim Seguin, *Robert Morris College*; Donald Shaw, *University of North Carolina*; Martin D. Sommernes, *Northern Arizona State University*; Linda Steiner, *Rutgers University*; Jill Diane Swensen, *Ithaca College*; Sharon Taylor, *Delaware State University*; Hazel Warlaumont, *California State University-Fullerton*; Richard Whitaker, *Buffalo State College*; Lynn Zoch, *University of South Carolina*.

*Special thanks from Richard Campbell:* I would also like to acknowledge the number of fine teachers at both the *University of Wisconsin-Milwaukee* and *Northwestern University* who helped shape the way I think about many of the issues raised in this book, and I am especially grateful to my former students at the *University of Wisconsin-Milwaukee, Mount Mary College*, the *University of Michigan, Middle Tennessee State University*, and my current students at *Miami University*. Some of my students have contributed directly to this text, and thousands have endured my courses over the years—and made them better. My all-time favorite former students, Chris Martin and Bettina Fabos, are now essential coauthors, as well as the creators of our book's Instructor's Resource Manual, Test Bank, and the *About the Media* DVD. I am grateful for Chris and Bettina's fine writing, research savvy, good stories, and tireless work amid their own teaching schedules and writing careers, all while raising two spirited daughters. I remain most grateful, though, to the people I most love: my son, Chris; my daughter, Caitlin; and, most of all, my wife, Dianna, whose line editing, content ideas, daily conversations, shared interests, and ongoing support are the resources that make this project go better with each edition.

*Special thanks from Christopher Martin and Bettina Fabos:* We would also like to thank Richard Campbell, with whom it is always a delight working on this project. We also appreciate the great energy, creativity, and talent that everyone at Bedford/St. Martin's brings to the book. From edition to edition, we also receive plenty of suggestions from *Media and Culture* users and reviewers and from our own journalism and media students. We would like to thank them for their input and for creating a community of sorts around the theme of critical perspectives on the media. Most of all, we'd like to thank our daughters, Olivia and Sabine, who bring us joy and laughter every day, and a sense of mission to better understand the world of media and culture in which they live.

Please feel free to email us at **mediaandculture@bedfordstmartins.com** with any comments, concerns, or suggestions!

# Contents

## WORDS AND PICTURES

## THE BUSINESS OF MASS MEDIA

## DEMOCRATIC EXPRESSION AND THE MASS MEDIA

Media ownership **affects the media you consume and how you receive that media.**

While the media used to be owned by numerous different companies, today six large conglomerates — **Sony, Disney, Comcast/NBC Universal, News Corp., Time Warner, and CBS** — dominate. This visualization breaks down the media holdings of these companies to help you understand their widespread influence:

• The six companies are ranked by how much they made in 2010, from the most revenue to the least.

• Seven areas of the media are represented in these charts: movies, broadcast TV, cable TV, books, newspapers, magazines, music, and radio.

• Each company is color-coded so you can easily track what it owns and where it ranks across each industry. For example, Time Warner owns *Rizzoli & Isles*, the top cable show, and *People*, the top magazine.

As you look at this visualization, think about how much of your daily media consumption is owned by these corporations. Which companies have the most influence on your news and entertainment intake? What does it mean that so few companies own so much of the media?

## The Top Companies and How Much $$ They Made in 2010

### Sony
**$90 billion**
Produces much of your music collection — and the devices you use to play it

### Disney
**$38.1 billion**
From movies to television, Disney owns a lot of what you watch

### Comcast/NBCU
**$35.8 billion**
Owns many favorite TV shows, and the cable system that delivers them

### News Corp.
**$32.8 billion**
Controls much of the daily news cycle — on cable TV and in newspapers

### Time Warner
**$26.9 billion**
Promotes its movies in its magazines — synergy at its best

### CBS Corporation
**$14 billion**
Plays a big part in your prime-time (broadcast TV) and drive-time (radio) hours

# How much do media companies make, really?

$553,000,000,000
◀ $553 billion Department of Defense proposed budget for 2011

$90,000,000,000
◀ $90 billion Sony's 2010 revenue

$85,000,000,000
◀ $85 billion Amount of 2008 U.S. government loan to insurance giant AIG

$74,230,000,000
◀ $74.23 billion Libya's Gross Domestic Product (GDP) in 2010

$56,000,000,000
◀ $56 billion Net worth of Bill Gates in 2011

$50,000,000,000
◀ $50 billion Facebook's reported value in 2011

$38,100,000,000
◀ $38.1 billion Disney's 2010 revenue

$32,800,000,000
◀ $32.8 billion News Corp.'s 2010 revenue

$29,300,000,000
◀ $29.3 billion Google's 2010 revenue

$28,200,000,000
◀ $28.2 billion President's fiscal year budget for the U.S. Department of Justice in 2011

$26,900,000,000
◀ $26.9 billion Time Warner's 2010 revenue

$18,700,000,000
◀ $18.7 billion NASA proposed budget for 2011

$18,600,000,000
◀ $18.6 billion Total U.S. retail sales in the videogame industry in 2010

$13,500,000,000
◀ $13.5 billion Net worth of Mark Zuckerberg (CEO of Facebook) in 2011

$13,400,000,000
◀ $13.4 billion Viacom's 2010 revenue

$10,600,000,000
◀ $10.6 billion Total U.S. movie box-office receipts in 2010

$9,000,000,000
◀ $9 billion Environmental Protection Agency proposed budget for 2011

$1,320,000,000
◀ $1.32 billion Worldwide gross for *Harry Potter and the Deathly Hallows Part 2*

$315,000,000
◀ $315 million Amount AOL paid for the *Huffington Post* in 2011

$100,000,000
◀ $100 million Estimated cost of the 2008 Beijing Olympics opening ceremony

$35,000,000
◀ $35 million Amount News Corp. sold MySpace for in 2011

$1,500,000
◀ $1.5 million Amount *People* magazine paid for the exclusive photos from Kim Kardashian's wedding

$142,544
◀ $142,544 Average four-year tuition and room and board at a private university

$50,221
◀ $50,221 Median U.S. household income in 2010